GO FISHING FOR

COD

GO FISHING FOR
COD

GRAEME PULLEN

The Oxford Illustrated Press

The Oxford Illustrated Press

© Graeme Pullen, 1989
Reprinted Twice 1990

ISBN 0 946609 66 7

Published by:
The Oxford Illustrated Press Limited, Haynes Publishing Group,
Sparkford, Nr Yeovil, Somerset BA22 7JJ, England.

Haynes Publications Inc., 861 Lawrence Drive, Newbury Park, California
91320, USA.

Printed in England by:
J.H. Haynes & Co Limited, Sparkford, Nr Yeovil, Somerset.

British Library Cataloguing in Publication Data
Pullen, Graeme
  Go fishing for cod.
  1. Great Britain. Coastal waters. Cod. Angling –
  Manuals
  I. Title
  799.1'758
  ISBN 0-946609-66-7

Library of Congress Catalog Card Number
89–80215

Contents

Dedication

To the man who invented the
suction pump—ideal for lugworm
collecting.

Introduction

Of all the species of fish that swim around our coastline, possibly the best known is the cod. This is due no doubt to its popularity with the housewife. Personally, while I enjoy the occasional cod in batter and chips in folds of newspaper and with gallons of vinegar, it comes second to a cheeseburger for flavour. I imagine much of the flavour of well cooked fish comes from the addition of various other ingredients. I often wonder with the basically bland taste of cod, whether we wouldn't be better if we dumped the fish and just sat down to a meal of the flavourings. This is a slightly biased view perhaps from a non-fish-eating fisherman, and I accept the fact that cod is established as part of our diet.

If ever we had a national sea fish I imagine the cod might be it. Everybody has heard of it, most anglers have encountered one, and both the beach and the boat angling fraternity contain a group of hard-core cod fishing specialists. It cannot surely be classed as a rip-roaring fighting fish, but it is present in enough numbers to make its pursuit worthwhile. I once had a letter from Frank Woolner, the editor of *Saltwater Sportsman* in the United States. He described our East Coast cod, as 'an engine block with a wiggle'! That's as close a description as I have ever heard. I would class this species as the British national fish of the winter, with the bass being the summer species.

Cod can be caught right around our coastline all year, but numbers fluctuate from area to area during the autumn and winter months, which makes fishing for them more successful. They are not a difficult fish to hook, entice into taking a bait, or gaff into the boat. But they grow to a very respectable size, and being so prolific must surely be one of the best 'big' fish to try if you are a beginner. They can be classed as a bottom-feeding fish, or a deep-water fish, but only in the context of depths within the continental shelf that surrounds us. Once out over the edge of this shelf the bottom contours drop away to the abyssal depths, where much is still to be learned, and where commercial fishing is still in the experimental stage. This shelf can be over two hundred miles from the land mass, and is home to most of our coastal species like haddock, cod and whiting. Where the water drops away, so light doesn't penetrate and the water temperature becomes markedly colder. There may well be cod down there, but until scientists confirm this I remain doubtful, and believe there are variant stocks of semi-resident fish on the areas of shelf itself.

They must be considered a cold-water fish, which is probably why the shore fishing for them is better around our coastline during the winter months. Then the sea surface temperatures start to drop and fishing from the shore comes into its own. While temperature, depths, food availability and salinity all play a part in the distribution of any species, I feel it is the plankton-rich waters of the Arctic that provide the basis of the cod fisheries in the northern hemisphere. The young of the herring and sprat, more commonly referred to as whitebait also form part of the diet of the cod, and these shoals are prolific off the coast of Norway and in the Baltic Sea. Cod are both

When pumping in that shore cod, keep him coming all the time to avoid the lead snagging if fishing over rough ground. Take care to also spread the line evenly on the spool for the following cast.

Introduction

scavengers and predators, and will follow the easiest supply of migratory food, much like the predators of the African plains follow the vast herds on their migration paths.

Human intervention in this fine balance of predator/prey can cause untold damage to those stocks, as can be seen in the over-exploitation of many of our commercial food fish. Today, the methods of locating and catching a species are so far advanced that it can literally be called the high-tech age of fishing. Electronic fish-finding equipment can pinpoint the biggest shoals of species most likely to bring the highest financial yield, and scoop them up completely. Instead of selective fishing of a certain year-class of fish, an entire shoal is wiped out, which leaves fewer fish in mature condition to replenish the stocks. In other words, we are catching them faster than they can reproduce.

Cod are not found in the warmer waters of the equator or less than 40° north, and can be caught up to 120 fathoms deep. Undoubtedly the larger specimens live up near the Arctic Circle where they have been netted to over a hundred pounds.

They reach a staggering size and the British rod-caught record is a little over 50 lb. It is difficult to define an average size, as that depends on locality, food supply and the size of the fish in the school. As for coloration some theories suggest that differences in colour marking are due to the different strains or 'races' of cod rather than any regional environment. While I agree that there may indeed be different 'races' in the northern hemisphere, I feel coloration can be dictated by the environment in which the cod live. On the sandy bottoms of the East Coast shallow beaches you get a light brown coloration. Once you move south and round to the west coast peninsula of Cornwall they get a deeper gold, even bronze colour to their flanks. Then if you move further north up to Scotland they develop a deep rusty colour. Off the coast of Ireland I have taken such cod in amongst thick kelp seaweed and general snaggy ground that have come up almost red with a sheen of dark brown over the back. These fish, usually in the 3–8 lb range, I believe are semi-resident, working the area amongst the rough ground and feeding on crabs and crustaceans. When the feeding is good they obviously stay within that area. Other anglers feel their colour is due

9

to the fact that they feed almost entirely on crabs. A similarity can be drawn between diets here, as salmon anglers often believe the pinkest flesh of the salmon comes when they have been feeding exclusively on prawns. I think it has nothing to do with the diet, but is the fish's natural reaction of the pigment in its skin to best blend in with the surrounding environment.

A tip for shark anglers is that the cod has a liver with a very high oil content for a whitefish. Some of us may remember being force-fed cod-liver oil tablets as youngsters.

If you are a shark angler and are out on a bottom-fishing trip in winter, try this. On gutting your catch of cod, take along a couple of plastic boxes, then simply drop in the cod's livers and pop them in the freezer when you get home. The plastic boxes lend themselves nicely to stacking in a freezer, and you will have something to start the shark season with, when rubby dubby may be scarce. You can buy cod liver oil extract, but keeping fresh livers makes it less costly.

Cod liver oil is well known for its medicinal qualities, and it was believed years ago to be good for easing pulmonary problems. In the commercial fishing world of yesteryear, before the age of high-tech electronics, the old trawlermen used to place some cod's liver in a metal tin, and then stand the tin on the boiler in the engine room. The heat from the boiler soon sent the oil to the surface where it was skimmed off and used for rubbing into their sea boots in order to keep the leather soft and pliable. The smell of those boots must have been dreadful, and I can't imagine the oily slick left on the pavements on rainy nights, but I guess soft boots were better than hard.

It has been suggested that the ceiling weight of commercially caught cod is in excess of 200 lb. I find this hard to believe, but remember the deep-water cod fleets operate in water and depths that cannot be reached by the angler using rod and line from a traditional charter boat. The best chance of a cod in excess of 60 lb must come from the areas of greatest food availability. I think therefore that the deep offshore wrecks may just harbour a fish of this weight or larger. I have heard enough stories of anglers hooking big fish that crash-dived straight into the tangled superstructure of the wreck, to believe they may not be the pollock, coalfish or small porbeagle shark they are thought to be. Many big cod are landed each year from charter boats operating over the wrecks, and the wrecks in the north of Scotland must be where the monster cod lurk.

This was confirmed by the small boat anglers who really revolutionised artificial lure fishing for cod from the lochs like the Firth of Clyde. Up until that time, pirking, as it is known, was

An angler waits expectantly from a shore mark for the codling to move in. Last light and a flood tide are the best conditions for winter codding, especially after a good blow.

previously only used for codling, haddock and coalfish by the charter boats operating in the north of England. From the mark known as the Gantocks came reports of three anglers making tremendous hauls of cod, not just bags of fish, but with individual specimens up to a new British record weight (at the time) of 46 lb. Soon this small area was under pressure not only from hordes of other anglers, but from the commercials who took an active interest. Once they started to move in the death knell sounded for the famed Gantocks cod. But it was at least an indication of the size Scottish cod could reach. Combine this with my own belief that the best fish feed towards the north, and you begin to realise the potential that must surely be waiting on the seabed around the many wrecks left by two world wars.

The population density of the north of Scotland means there is no intensive charter fishing industry to capitalise on the wrecks in the deep water offshore. Add unattractive weather conditions, and you begin to see it's time somebody launched an expedition up there.

The cod seem to migrate south from the Arctic around September. They are thickest off the south coast of England from the end of November until January, so it is worth considering that October to November might be the months that the big fish are closest to those wrecks off the north of Scotland. Because you would be fishing in very deep water, and with possibly harsh tidal conditions, I think you would need a good 50-lb standup rod and shoulder harness, with pirks at least a foot or more long, and weighing up to two pounds. The monster cod will not be nosing about the seabed looking for a three-inch lugworm, but will be after anything of a pound or larger that can fit in its mouth. Until somebody tries wrecking off the north of Scotland in the winter, I cannot see the British rod-caught record going much over 55 lb.

Codling are generally regarded as smaller fish, though at which stage of its life a codling becomes a cod is unknown. The term codling I have seen applied to a fish of 10 lb and that I would almost certainly classify as a fully grown fish. In my mind a codling can be called a cod when it reaches a weight of about 3 lb. If they weigh under one pound they can be called codlets, and anything under four ounces is a fish finger! It's hard to become conservation minded with this species as it

Introduction

is such a primary food source and is not under direct threat of extinction, although commercial fishing must surely be taking its toll on stocks. When the fishing in winter is at its peak the level of codling can be tiresome if you are out in a boat expecting a twenty-pounder. Yet that same fish when caught from the shore by a fish-starved beach angler is like winning the pools. You have to learn to respect fish of all sizes, despite what you think it should weigh. If we all caught the size of fish we wanted the excitement of the unknown would disappear.

Cod are prime white-fleshed eating fish. In most angling circles you would be deemed a bit short in the brain department if you put them back alive, as it would be like emptying the cash register over the side. However, I respect the individual views of each angler, and if your mind is set on the preservation of the species through conservation

This cod landed by the writer gives an indication of what it had been feeding on when it coughed up these shrimps. Cod are prolific rubbish eaters and scavenge most things on the bottom.

then by all means return fish. What I should point out, however, is that those fish returned, with the exception of beach-caught fish, have little chance of survival. They have a swim bladder, and when pumped up to the surface blow up with air and are unable to swim back down if released. Some species can have this air bladder punctured by a sharp ice-pick which pops the air bag just behind the pectoral fin. I have done this with 50-lb amberjacks off wrecks in Florida, and it has been proved by tagging that they will survive. Even when that air bladder is pierced, however, the cod can't muster enough strength to get back down to the sea bed, and is simply swept away on the tide. It is better to keep them for eating, than see them go to waste due to misguided conservation efforts. If you catch more than you can eat or freeze down, either find a market for them or simply give them away to friends and relatives.

The cod has a considerable appetite and will eat almost anything. In the 1960s when there was great interest in wire line fishing around the Isle of Wight, cod were caught with plastic cups inside them. I myself took a fish off a Norfolk beach which on being gutted later was found to contain a plastic cup. The plastic cups were the white disposable types used on ships and liners. Unfortunately it became obvious that they were disposing of them by dumping over the side rather than on land. The plastic cups sank to the bottom, and rolled around on the tide until the cod came across them. One can only imagine that they mistook them for squid. The fact that they eat plastic perhaps confirms what I have already said about their prodigious appetite. Although there are a few times when they will be preoccupied on small crabs or shrimps, the chances are better if you have anchored a large bait out where they can find it.

Shore Fishing

Shore fishing for cod is often thought to be a 'chuck-it-and-chance-it' affair. While a good number of cod, some of them large, do fall for a degree of unsophistication, more will be landed by the fisherman who attaches a bit more thought to his approach. For the shore fisherman, seasons dictate the times he is most likely to catch cod. In the far north of England, and Scotland, there are rock venues dropping away into deep water where they can be taken with some degree of regularity right throughout the year. Once you get further south where the water depths close to shore start to shallow up, the cod stocks thin out.

Once you get into an area south of a line drawn from say, North Wales to the Wash, the cod are very predictable in putting in an appearance in any sort of numbers. The time to start hoping for them would be around the second week of October when they make a showing along the Suffolk beaches. They peak here from the middle to the end of October, and then drift away a bit. The next showing of cod comes from Rye to Dungeness on the south-east coast in mid-November. They stay in large numbers for about a month then thin out in January. Further along the coast at Eastbourne in Sussex they peak from the end of November until the end of December. Then they too thin out. December to January can see very big shore cod taken from the steep shingle beaches of Chesil and the like off the Dorset coast. Basically any time from mid-October to the end of January is a good time for shore codding, but remember that the Bristol Channel rock marks and many of the South Wales shore

15

Go Fishing for Cod

Bagshot beach angler
Paul Rivers holds
Graeme Pullen's 9 lb 5 oz
fish that tried to eat a
dab hooked on light tackle

marks yield runs of winter and spring cod. These fish will stay on until April, running far up the Channel, and remaining a viable proposition for the angler prepared to sit it out with a big bait.

It's best to break your shore cod fishing down into categories. There are those fish that come from the wide open shallow sandy beaches of the east coast—north Norfolk, Suffolk, the Thames Estuary and Rye. From Deal round to Eastbourne you have fairly steep shingle beaches, but still with a heavy run of tide. Chesil Beach in Dorset would mark the end of shingle beaches, and the Bristol Channel marks, like those of the north of England would be classed as 'rough ground' fishing.

Shore Fishing

Fishing from Sandy Beaches

Many anglers shun the east coast cod beaches of Norfolk and Suffolk because they are desolate in winter and, being shallow, they think you have to cast at least 150 yards with a bait. While I have to agree with the first point, the population density is less in desolate areas, so there is more chance of getting a good shore mark to yourself. The second point is just wrong! The importance of all shore fishing can be related to two things—understanding of tidal conditions and where the food is going to be, and the careful presentation of fresh hookbait. I've fished at 90 yards with freshly dug lugworm against a top angler winding out poor lug 130 yards and fished them inside out. I cannot stress too strongly the importance of using as fresh a bait as you can

The author admires a fine cod taken on lugworm from the flat beaches of Norfolk. Noting the times at which other anglers catch their fish will generally help when fishing the following day.

17

lay your hands on. While cod do have the reputation of being vacuum cleaners of the seabed, they are more likely to pick up fresh bait than stale.

What you must do with these shallow beaches is to walk them at low tide springs. That is when the tide is out at its farthest point. What you are looking for is a slight indentation in the seabed about 80–120 yards out from the high tide mark. Even a small depression in the surrounding desert-like seascape will be a wash-around area for loose particles of food. The cod move along the coast and will obviously stop in this area longer, giving you a better chance. If you simply cannot get to the venue to coincide with low tide conditions you have to look for two other signs. The first and easiest is to look laterally along the beachline to see the level of sand deposited between the breakers. During each storm, varying amounts of sand or shingle are thrown up by the action of the surf. One set of breakers will always be a bit higher than another, so what you are looking for is the highest bank of sand or shingle over six or seven sets of breakers. While it is often thought that the deepest water between breakers at high tide means deep water out in front of you, the reverse is in fact true. Any sand deposited at high water will not be out in front of you so at high water you must surely have a greater depression in front of you, and thereby a food trap.

The other sign to look for was first shown to me properly by Joe Malat, a professional shore guide who ran a four-wheel-drive vehicle on the Outer Banks of North Carolina. Here the fishing was from level sand beaches where the best fishing was located by looking for sloughs. A slough is a natural break in the wave pattern, which you look for just as the wave is starting to crest. If you look along the surfline and see a section that isn't surfing, then you know the water is deeper there. A surfline is caused by a wave travelling by natural momentum over hundreds of miles, affected only by the wind. It then hits the friction of the seabed as the water becomes shallow, which means the lower end drags while the crest topples, almost like tripping over. When the water is deeper the wave will not crest.

The Outer Banks guides charge up to $200 for a day with their services, and they watch for the tiniest detail to put their clients on the fish. Since I was shown a proper slough, fished it, and landed red drum and bluefish from it, I have learned to apply the same approach to shore codding. The red drum and cod are not dissimilar, in that they both have the underslung mouths of bottom feeders. They won't punch through a bank of waves like bass or bluefish, so you need to look for anything that will create a 'feature' or holding point for food items. The same applies to shallow sandy beaches. You should walk along them or scan them with binoculars until you see that natural break in the wave pattern, through which the fish pass from the offshore sandbank to feed in the littoral zone close in. The littoral zone is the area just behind where the waves draw back, where most food items are likely to wash around.

Once you have located the slough or wave gap you need to fish a bait on the uptide side or edge of it. Off the east coast the tide run can be considerable, and you will also have the wind to contend with. Judge your cast carefully and place your bait on the uptide dropoff of that edge or slough. You may not be able to reach the break as the tide pushes you up the beach. But don't worry, take a bearing off the land behind you so that if you lose the wave pattern at extreme high water, you can still line up a cast to place the bait in a line with the 'door' through the offshore sandbank the cod will be using.

At high water it is often worth dropping a cast in short to fish the downstream end of the breakers (the food breakers). Food items washed up to the high tide line will be sucked around the edge and any cod swimming into the tidal flow will be attracted by this trickle of food. This is a tip worth remembering when you are scratching around to find fish at the beginning and end of the main cod runs. You need to have a good eye for such features if you fish the wide flat sand beaches.

Another tip that has given me some success is this. Watch, or ask, to discover when other anglers have taken their fish. Very often something in the tidal conditions switches the fish on, and they run the gap in the wave pattern together. I have had codling as soon as the lead has gripped bottom, and equally quickly they have switched off and an angler farther down the beach has taken them. It's easy to work out which way they are running, but a good general guide is that they will run through the breaker gap then feed into the tide. This gives them greatest scent coverage with the single barbel under their chin, which helps them obtain food. By making a mental note of when the fish have been on the bite, you should be able to return at the next tide, at exactly the same spot, but an hour later as the tide gets later each day. It's rare, once you have established the pattern, not to catch fish at the same state of the tide the following day. This only works when the weather conditions remain the same, and a shift in wind may alter the surfline patterns. If the conditions do remain the same you can generally bank on taking fish like this for around four days. I can vouch for this, having spent up to four consecutive tides on various Norfolk beaches!

Pretty much the same rigs can be used for both sand and shingle beaches. You can use a running paternoster, a fixed paternoster with a single snood, or a multiple paternoster with several hooks. It all depends on how much bait you have. On the sandy beaches lugworm will be the bait to dominate catches, and assuming you have an almost endless supply of them, use the paternoster with three snoods. Obviously the amino-acid scent trail percolating along the seabed from three worm baits has a greater chance of being discovered than a single worm. The ground will be almost snag-free so you shouldn't lose gear. The only time, other than a crack-off, when you will lose gear is at low tide, when a big surf is running. You can cast out as far as you can, but unknown to you, the surf may be carrying a lot of sand in suspension. It will then bury your end gear—which of course you don't discover until you try to retrieve. The only way to minimise gear loss is by wading out as far as possible, pointing the rod at the lead and walk backwards, having screwed the reel drag down first. It is better to break your line as near the lead as possible and thus reduce the chances of that loose line creating a snag. The hooks will soon rust away, but alas nylon monofilament is with us a lifetime. Most lines should break at the shock leader knot, so you only lose that, and not fifty yards of main line.

When fishing the flat beaches I would advise the use of baitclips, although I have found no requirement to blast a bait out 130 yards. Not only does it streamline the bait to get those extra few yards if you are a mediocre caster, but it prevents the worm bait either blowing up the snood or breaking up altogether. A good second bait would be peeler crab.

There really is no substitute for fresh bait. Even if you dig worms, try to paper them down and toughen them for use as soon after digging as possible.

A final word on sandy beaches; never be afraid to move right or left several hundred yards in an effort to find the fish. If you cannot get there at low tide to check out the ground, or if you don't have a high bank of sand between the groynes to tell you there is extra depth, or if you cannot see a slough in the surfline, move about trying to find a few fish. If you catch nothing on that first session, don't write the area off as being useless. Try further along, or further back until you pick up something. Fish can be fickle creatures and rarely hang themselves on the hooks!

Go Fishing for Cod

Fishing from Shingle Beaches

Catching cod from steeper shingle beaches is basically similar except that you will be unable to see any break in the surfline. You will already have deeper water in front of you, and tidal conditions may be much stronger.

From Rye round to Dungeness, many thousands of shore anglers fish the early winter cod, and apply a different approach to searching out the better fish. Here you will need to get the bait no more than eighty yards or so out to be in with as much chance as the next chap. What you will need is a lead that anchors a big juicy bunch of lugworm in that strong tide, so the cod can locate it easily. For this I use only one type of rig: a single-snood paternoster, with a long two-foot snood, and a double-hook rig at the end. You need to thread at least three good lugworms up the first hook, over the eye and up the line a few inches. Then the second hook is slid down and the first worm nicked through the end. This not only holds the worms securely for the cast, but it also acts as a hooking device.

I was first told about the advantages of the double-hook rig many years ago by Jim Ingledew, a famous East Coast cod angler, who drove all the way from Peterborough just to spend a session on the Norfolk and Suffolk beaches. At that time only a few anglers were using double-hook rigs, and then it was only to hold out the bait so it didn't bunch up on the cast. Jim was the first to realise that the angle at which the bait lay in the tide meant that the top or 'holder' hook actually hooked a higher percentage of cod. Whether you are a long caster or not I think you should employ a baitclip for a big bunch of worms like this. You can clip your bait either snood up or snood down, but if it is clipped down you can gain from the slipstream effect of the lead during the cast.

The tide run on a steep shingle beach will be either right-to-left or vice-versa. On busy beaches where there are a lot of anglers, there is always someone who doesn't use a grip lead, and finds his tackle dragging round in the tide to tangle with several other anglers downtide. We should all forgive mistakes once, even twice perhaps, but a persistent culprit should have either a copy of this book shoved up his jumper, or his line cut!

Shore Fishing

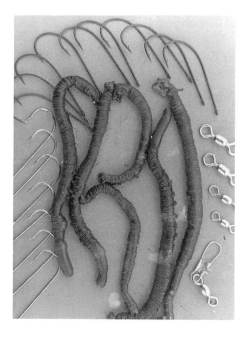

Prime Black lugworm, gutted and ready to be hooked. Use a strong wire hook for black lug or peeler as it shouldn't straighten out under the pressure of a big fish. Although poor fighters, a big cod still has the body weight to use in the tidal flow to straighten out hooks.

To fish steep tidal beaches effectively you should clip your bait up ready to make the cast, then walk uptide for about thirty yards. Make your cast straight out in front of you, but instead of dropping the reel in gear, allow it to free spool with the tidal flow as you walk back to your rod rest. Knock the reel in gear and the line should pull tight in the flow and the tip of the rod pull over. You always use a lead where the wires break out, but in extreme tidal conditions you need a nose-wired lead with long arms so that the tide, and sometimes accumulations of weed, cannot trip the wires. What you should get is known as a slack-line bite. The cod comes along, following the scent trail of amino acids laid down by that glorious bunch of juicy lugworms. He locates them, engulfs the lot and turns away to start looking for more. He pulls up against the grip lead with its wires buried in the sand and feels a tug. That's your first indication of a bite, when the rod top pulls down sharply. At the bait end the cod, now a bit alarmed at the restriction, bolts off and pulls the hooks in, while the lead drags across the bottom holding the tension on those same hooks. This breaks the tension of the tide acting on the line, and

23

you get what is known as a slack-liner. The initial rod top jab is followed by a spring back of the tip, and the line falls slack in the water. The first thing to do is grab the rod as the fish is already hooked. Then wind down fast as the cod will be dropping downtide and may run into either snags, groynes or the next angler's line. Once you get all the stretch out of the line, give the rod a good thump backwards while you walk smartly back up the beach. That should drive the hooks in past the barb. Then with a pump and wind action bring the fish in towards the surfline.

My first initiation into a slack-liner bite was on one of the Norfolk beaches. I had a pair of rods fishing lug about ninety yards out, and it was low tide with the first of the flood just started. About a hundred yards to my left were Jim Ingledew and his partner Brian Flack. After the initial excitement I became bored, and setting the drags on the reels so line could be pulled off under pressure, I set off for a chat with Jim. As I stood talking Brian suddenly shouted, 'Hey boy, you've got a slack-liner!' I was amazed at how he could see what was happening to my rod at over a hundred yards, but what he had seen of course was the pair of rod tips bowed over in silhouette against the sky. When one stood straight and the other still curved it was obvious to him I had a cod. I started back with a slow casual walk, which developed into a full cavalry charge, splashing through the water, as I could see all the line washing around the monopod! I duly landed that fish, which if I recall correctly was over $8^{1}/_{2}$ lb! I didn't deserve it of course, but it made up for all those other fish I thought I did deserve but didn't catch!

The exception to this anchored bait rule on steep beaches, is at slack high or slack low tide. Then you can change to an unwired straight bomb and allow the bait to roll around slightly. You can also use this tidal period to rig with a three-hook paternoster, using a single worm on a single hook. This method has given me a few good codling when I was not really expecting a lot of fish. As I have said, you never really know when the cod are going to come, so be prepared to experiment a bit. I know of anglers who just leave their rods in until the tide starts to move, but I'm a firm believer that it's a bait in the water that catches the fish, no matter what the state of the tide.

Shore Fishing

This big cod held by the author just shows you never know how big the fish is that takes your bait. He was regularly catching two pound fish when this monster came along.

Go Fishing for Cod

Big cod are very much a predatory as well as a scavenging fish, feeding freely on crustaceans, shrimps and any small fish they can catch. Even during daytime there can be little daylight getting through to the seabed, and I can only assume they locate these fish by noises given off during their feeding, or by sensory receptors in their lateral line. In the early seventies at big shore cod venues like Dungeness in Kent, a good many anglers had a tiny rattling bite, followed by a big slack-line bite, and a missed fish. Those initial nibbles were from the voracious whiting, which run the same seasons and grounds as the cod. It wasn't until anglers started to leave those 'nibbling' bites alone, and just watched the rod tops, that they began to realise the whiting chewing away at their worm baits were being snaffled by big cod! A few were landed on small whiting rigs, but many more were missed.

It then occurred to the anglers to develop a new rig that would allow them to fish these same whiting as a livebait. Winter whiting probably average six ounces to half a pound and are almost impossible to cast. Admittedly they could be lobbed out thirty or forty yards on a big fixed spool outfit, but anything more powerful attempted with a good beachcaster and multiplier reel was courting disaster in the shape of exploding bird's nests! Big baits are notoriously difficult to cast, and to fish them at distance as a livebait is impossible. The impact of both the cast and hitting the water usually kills any livebait instantly. The cod men came up with the idea of whipping a larger single hook, unbaited, a couple of inches above the worm-baited whiting hook. When the whiting came along and gobbled up the worm, the anglers left him to hook himself against the grip lead, which of course he was too small to break out. That way they knew they could fish a livebait for an unlimited time secure in the knowledge that the only bite they were likely to get would be from a big old 'lunker' cod. This method still applies, but I would advise its use only in the waters that produce double-figure fish with some sort of regularity. While a 5-lb cod probably does have a go at immature whiting, it is likely to pass up any tethered offering if it is more than half a pound in weight.

While a good many beach men feel it is only the whiting that are taken by cod, I feel it is worth leaving any small fish moored out in the tidal flow. Surely cod come across a myriad of immature species while grubbing their way across the bottom, and a blenny, pouting or poor cod are just as likely to be thrown down the hatch as a whiting. It is true that during the peak runs of cod and whiting around the south-east of England in the months of November and December, the whiting are in so thick that this is the prime source of live fish food a cod comes across. Much as they glut themselves on the sprats of the Thames estuary during the month of January, so the cod will cash in on any whiting boom.

I once took a $9^1/_2$-lb cod off the Martello tower on Langney Point beachfront at Eastbourne, that had to be after a dab I had left out hooked. I was only using tiny blued Aberdeen match hooks in my search for some soles, and had found the dab population of the area more than obliging with my half-lugworm offerings. At 4 am after watching a twittering bite on my Conoflex tip it folded over and almost left the monopod! I have had similar occurrences when fishing mini-baits on small hooks, and had previously put the bite down to a hit-and-run bass. Sometimes the hooks came back straight, so the species were of reasonable size. I now believe those bites were from big cod, and when fishing for dabs and small fish at a time of year likely to see a big cod, I now whip on a larger hook above the bait. Most of the time I catch nothing, but should a 'lunker' engulf your whiting or dab, you will at least be in with a chance of landing it.

With most steep stone beaches the constant scouring action of the tide means there will be few features on the sea bed. It can still be worthwhile walking the area you intend to fish at low water springs, marking down either mentally or in a small notebook features which might attract cod. Mussel beds are a prime feeding area, although they can give you heavy losses on terminal gear. Collect a few and hold them on your hook with elasticated thread. It always seems best to fish near the edge of the mussel beds, not because you reduce your tackle losses, although that helps, but to isolate your bait near a positive food source. Crabs love mussel beds and will soon strip a worm clean, leaving you looking at a baitless hook.

Another good feature is an outcrop of rocks or big boulders. Try to get landmarks from your high-water casting position to establish where they will be at high water, then aim to fish a bait at the edge of

It is always worth checking out the low-tide beach area before you start to fish. You can then make a mental note of any depressions or sandbars that might aid catches like this mixed bag taken by the author.

A brace of cod from the most famous shore mark of all time. Dungeness beach in Kent is a shadow of its former self but when conditions are right it can still give a hint of what fishing used to be like in the 1960s.

Go Fishing for Cod

that area. Sewer outfalls, although unsavoury places to fish, invariably have a big steel pipe running out to sea. The pipe itself may be a feature on a tractless void of sand and it could be well worth fishing near one. As well as the usual crabs, the rich nutrients being discharged by the pipe will be an attraction to shrimps, prawns and other small fish harbouring around it. Try to fish a bait on the downtide side of each feature, then if you get trouble with weed dragging or breaking out the grip leads, you won't lose your terminal gear in the snag.

On steep shingle beaches, the one thing that seems to kill all fishing for cod is a flat calm with an easterly airflow. Easterlies generally make the water go clear, and for some reason this puts the cod off, although you would think they found it easier to locate their food. I assume the olfactory or smell senses are their primary food location device though surely a scent is just as strong in clear water. It is a strange phenomenon, but certainly worth noting if you have a long drive to the venue. These same beaches will invariably be at their peaks after a good westerly, south-westerly or even southern blow. The gales stir up the food, and the littoral zone, so close to the surfline in usual conditions, will be spread out to sea further by the action of the undertow. I would suggest the best of the fishing for cod is after a good 24-hour gale from this quarter, as soon as the wind begins to abate.

While lugworm predominates in cod catches from open, shallow, sandy beaches, areas of small shingle and stones will be better for peeler crab and squid. There will be a proliferation of crabs around the features of mussel beds, rocks and pipes. These in turn rarely thin out until the first really heavy frosts of January, so with plenty of crab about the cod will use them as a major food supply. Close to shore, cod are unlikely to come across any profusion of squid, so why this bait is a success is beyond me. Nevertheless it works, and should be tried if you want better than average fish.

Shore Fishing

Fishing from Rocks

The third type of shore fishing is rock fishing. This involves really snaggy ground, where virtually every cast means a mortality in the tackle box. If you are new to an area you are going to lose an awful lot of gear, and I strongly advise you to contact either a local angler or a club to learn some of the better areas. But the rougher the ground the more likely there is going to be a food supply sheltering there. Where there is a food supply, the cod will not be a million miles away. As a travelling fishing writer it is a problem I am only too well aware of. When writing up a feature on a venue I have never fished before, the first thing I do is to phone some sort of local expert, and pick his brains. Better still I get him to go with me, and that way I am sure of being in the right place.

If you are fishing somewhere like the Bristol Channel, with its enormous rise and fall of tide, you need to fish at low water. The tide will almost certainly be covering snaggy slate-bed rocks at high water, and even at half ebb or flood you may be unable to reach clean ground. Even if you do, the chances of your lead or fish snagging in a rock crevice is pretty high. This means you will need to fish at low-water periods, rather than spending time researching the ground.

The best way to do this if you are unable to find a local contact is by casting the area with just a plain bomb, with no hooks at all. You should be able to feel whether the lead is bumping over sand, tapping against rock, or pulling into kelp beds. Nearly all the low-water marks in the Bristol Channel right down to south-west Wales and north Cornwall and North Devon will see your lead on sand. That is where the cod will be running through, and should you get a low-water spring tide coinciding with the hours of first darkness, you should have an excellent chance of a big cod. This type of venue will definitely be better for the angler who can throw the lead a long way, simply because he will get in more 'bait-time' than an inferior caster. Basically anyone who can throw a big bait seventy yards should have a chance of a cod at one of these low-water rock marks. But remember what I said about cod moving down a stretch of beach, or into a feature area at certain stages of the tide. They may not necessarily run a beach directly at slack low water. They may run during the first hour of flood, and that is probably when you will get them. There are times when they will come three or even four hours after high water, and then the inferior caster will be unable to hold a bait out on the clean ground. If he can cast say, seventy or eighty yards at dead low water, and the first of the snags such as kelp beds or rocks are forty yards out, he will only just be putting his baits over clean ground after being pushed back twenty yards by an incoming tide. He also runs the risk then of hooking a fish and being unable to get it up off the bottom sufficiently to clear those snags on the way in. Nothing is more infuriating than to spend time, energy and money in procuring a good supply of bait, spending half an hour clambering over big boulders and rocks, fishing three hours then having a decent cod snag itself on the way in! I know, I've done it! Once the tide pushes you in another ten yards you cannot clear those snags, and might just as well pack up fishing. Infuriating factor number two then comes into play, as you sit and watch your friend, still planting his bait out over clean ground, and worse still . . . catching cod!

Cod taken from these rocky venues are likely to be large, somewhere around 5 lb or 8 lb average size, with an outside chance of a double-figure fish. Big cod need big baits, and it is here that the cocktail baits of two flavours seem to work best. I have no idea why, but the best big cod bait seems to be a lugworm and squid cocktail. The lugworms are threaded up the line first, preferably held in position with a second hook further up the trace. Then the squid strip, cut thinly, about the width of your middle finger, is threaded a couple of times over the bend. It can be bound down with elasticated cotton, using the eye of the hook as a base to tie to, then sliding the lugworm back down over the hook eye when complete. This kind of big bait will definitely need some form of baitclip, in order to maintain the quantity of bait hitting the water, but more important is to ensure you get those few extra vital yards that will put the bait out over clean sand.

Where there are rocky headlands there are bound to be tidal currents and you should use a break-out grip lead, with collapsible wires enabling you to fish during the first of the flood tide. It may also be beneficial to fit a vane that allows the lead to rise up off the bottom quickly on the retrieve and thus minimise tackle losses. There

Possibly the biggest shore fish that many anglers will catch, the cod needs a specialised approach if successful catches, like this specimen landed by the author, are to be obtained.

The advent of pirk fishing in the south of England has seen some outstanding catches. By changing size, shape and colour of the pirks, the angler has a useful array of weaponry in his arsenal.

Some of the best cod hooks come from Alan Bramley's factory in Redditch. 'Partridge', the John Holden Universal Hooks, are amongst the best for whiting, cod and other species taken from the shore.

Not only the shape but the colour of the pirk can make an important difference. The author took this double figure cod on a pirk painted fluorescent yellow.

A monster haul of cod by the deadly duo Bob Edwards (left) and Norman Message, from the famed small boat *4 Pints*. There have been occasions when they had so many double figure cod aboard that they couldn't get *4 Pints* up on the plane and had to ship half their catch to another dinghy!

This angler looks delighted with the double figure cod he has landed. When you have caught enough for your own needs, share the rest out among your fellow anglers. Such fine food should not be wasted.

Over the side comes a 20 lb cod landed by Derek Box from his Eastbourne-based dinghy. The fish took a strip of cuttlefish.

Above: Three men in a boat and a massive catch of big cod. Left to right, Graeme Pullen, Norman Message and Bob Edwards show an incredible mixed bag of cod, conger and even an angler fish, all taken from a rough ground mark not from a wreck. Each of the cod in the foreground topped the 20 lb barrier.

Left: The author took this nicely marked cod while fishing redgill artificial eel over pinnacle rocks in Ireland.

are some moulds about now that incorporate this vaned appearance, which when coupled to a high retrieve ratio reel, means you can minimise tackle losses, and increase the chance of getting the cod back in through the snags. Larger than average beach multipliers will be better for high gear ratios, and remember you must keep turning the reel handle as fast as possible whether a fish is on or not, to keep both lead and fish above the snags. As you wind, try to distribute the line at an even pressure across the reel spool, and spread it evenly. This may be difficult during the excitement of landing a fish, but it pays dividends in allowing you a trouble-free reel on the next cast. With a fishing period of just three or four hours you need all the seconds you can get when the fish are feeding. The only type of rough ground that I have been able to extract a snagged fish from is large boulders worn smooth by the rolling action of one boulder against another.

If you feel your lead snag solid on the way in and tugging at different angles can't free it, there are two things you can try. Firstly set the rod back in the rest or monopod and slacken off the tension. Don't let the line fall around in the surfline, but just ease off so it is slack to the tip. After getting its breath back a snagged fish will sometimes throb around and pull the lead in the opposite direction to you, thus freeing it. Once the rod top starts to bob around, tighten up the reel drag, wind down hard on the fish, and if possible, walk backwards as you wind, to keep it coming over the snags. But watch out behind you so that you don't disappear down a rock crevice!

The other alternative should only be used if your fish has snagged higher than the low-water mark, and only if you are fishing the full tidal period back down to low water again. Break or cut the line after taking it from the rod top, tie it to a boulder, and mark where you have tied it with either a heap of boulders or piece of wood. You can then retrieve both fish and terminal gear at low water, and continue fishing with a new terminal rig. One point worth noting. Make sure your next cast is downtide from the snagged line, otherwise any fish or gear you bring back in may tangle again with the loose line.

I managed to retrieve a fish and tackle in this way recently on a Sussex breakwater, when I had a cod snagged on the way in. The weed had built up on the line as my grip lead held it out in the tidal flow, and was dragging round slowly in the small shingle without the grip wires breaking out. As I started to pump the fish in I realised there would be a point when the tide would beat me to it, as it were, which it did and I snagged something on the breakwater. Despite rude remarks from my companions, I pulled as much as I dared to get line in. At this stage I could just see the white underbelly of a good cod in the light of my lamp. Taking the line from the rod top, I snapped it off and tied it around the breaker nearest me, then rigged up and fished on. At about half ebb I could climb out along the wooden pilings and managed to retrieve not only my terminal tackle, but a nice cod as well! While waiting for the tide to drop sufficiently for me to get to the fish, I landed a heap of whiting and pout, plus another two cod as well!

The only area where this fails to work is up in Scotland, where the shore men fish from very snaggy rock cliffs, and have no way of getting down to the fish. On no account is a cod worth risking your neck for by climbing down precarious rock marks. Deep-water marks close to steep cliffs can have dangerous ocean swells that build up quickly and can snatch you away in two seconds. Your friends will be unable to help you as they too would be risking themselves in a one-sided situation. Always treat the more dangerous fishing positions with respect. Even though you might lose the odd fish, you can at least return to fish another day.

The best terminal rig for such rough ground is either a 6 or 8 oz bomb, lobbed out as far as possible with a generous helping of either lugworm or mussel. This is best done at slack tide, and of course you make sure your rod blank is capable of throwing a heavy lead, and that you have a heavy shock leader to withstand the impact of the cast. Using a wire-free bomb for a lead you minimise the loss of tackle, for make no mistake, this kind of fishing can make vast inroads into your tackle stocks. Most of the anglers I know like to mould their own leads, and rig up terminal gear only with a large single-snood, single-hook paternosters. There is no point in using multi-hook rigs on ground like this, as it is going to be a bonus if you get everything back in one piece! Plain bombs can be used to best effect at slack waters, both high and low, but once the water starts to 'push' a bit, you'll find the lead being dragged round into snags. I

Shore Fishing

Once in a while the unusual happens. Graham Ward, a Kent matchman had the luck to hook this 24 lb Cod from the south-east cod mark of Kingsdown Butts, a monster fish rarely taken by most shore anglers in a lifetime of fishing.

usually fish the plain bomb until I lose that first set of gear, and then change to the fixed lead. This anchors the bait over what you regard as the cleanest piece of ground, but it puts the odds of snagging it up considerably. For this reason use a reel with a high gear ratio to keep the terminal gear up off the bottom. Generally with cliff and high rock marks, distance isn't too important. As long as you can poke it out over a bit of patchy or clean ground, you are likely to pick up a good sized cod.

There are two types of lead to use. It can be made either as a fixed wire lead, or with collapsible wires like a break-out lead. As you will not be putting your all into blasting a bunch of worms out to the horizon, you can dispense with the second bait-holding hook. That

43

Go Fishing for Cod

The magic of a perfect cod night. The wind has died after the storm, the surf tumbles in, and the beach sparkles with frost. You just *know* you are going to catch fish. Norman Message with a fine catch of Sussex shore cod taken from Pevensey Bay.

only adds to the problem of snagging up, and the lugworm should hold together for a 70–90 yard cast. Mussel, as I have said, can be a super rough ground bait, presumably because of its availability to the cod. It's soft though, and will need tying to the hookshank with elasticated thread. Again, dispense with the second bait-holding hook, but both mussel and lug will need support during the cast by a baitclip, preferably clipping it down near the lead.

Cod must be treated almost exclusively as a bottom-feeding species. The partially underslung mouth should be an indication of this. The barbule on the chin is another pointer to bottom feeders, and doubtless helps in the location of food items perhaps by smell or vibration. Although I have known them landed on calm seas and in clear water, it is so rare it must be deemed a freak capture. The two best times are during the hours of first darkness on a flooding tide, and just after a good blow with the wind having been in a south or south to south-westerly direction. During both sets of conditions from October through to February you are very likely to take a shore cod. The absolute optimum period is when the wind drops after a good blow, coinciding with a flooding evening tide. In November, in the last couple of weeks, I would almost put money on being able to produce a cod from the shore.

They can be landed to a huge size by beach anglers, certainly to 40 lb, but the beginner should be content with the average size codling of 3 lb or so. It's also worth noting that in recent years, the really big shore cod in excess of 25 lb, have been coming from rocky marks rather than the wide shallow east coast sand beaches. This is not due to an influx of cod into those areas, but an influx of cod anglers, who are just starting to capitalise on the latest innovations and technical advances made within the tackle trade.

New rod-building materials like carbon, kevlar and glass mixes coupled with new resin bondings have created fishing rods capable of withstanding considerable punishment when casting big baits. Reel makers like Shimano have now come up with models like the Speedmaster that have line-gobbling gear ratios, wheeling both your terminal gear, and we hope, cod, quickly away from the snags. Hookmakers like Partridge and Mustad have an almost endless supply of different models to choose from. Then you have the competitive world of monofilament line. Makers like Ande and Stren, Berkley and Sylcast all give good lines capable of hard wear under a wide variety of conditions. For supporting your rod you can buy monopods, bipods, tripods and T-rests, or you can take a welding torch, some scrap iron and create your own. I had a couple of monopods made up that are a devil to carry, but they have a 'stamping' iron in the front to drive them deep into the sand or shingle, from where they never move. They also add two feet to the height of the rod itself.

Of all the requirements for shore fishermen hoping to take a fish, bait should get top priority. You really need concentrate on just four: lugworm, squid, peeler crab and mussel, or you can make a cocktail of any of them. Even if you have mediocre tackle, are a poor caster and can only leave work after high tide, you still have a chance of a cod if you have a good fresh bait. The only other point to concentrate on is time and location. Don't waste your time scouring areas where a cod hasn't been seen for a decade. Stick to the type of areas mentioned, and always get some local knowledge first. Although they are often termed the 'swimming dustbin' for their prodigious appetite, they can also be fickle feeders, moving into a littoral area of beach zone only when the food content is at its highest.

And should you meet in a bar one evening, or one of those 'cod-aren't-worth-fishing-for-they're-too-easy-to-catch' types, tell him to pick up a beach outfit and try catching a few from the shore. It can be far more satisfying landing a smaller cod from the beach than a larger fish from a boat. You will have earned it entirely through your own efforts.

Boat Fishing

Boat fishing for this species can be far more productive in terms of the hours put in than shore fishing. Although at certain times of the season the cod will nose right into three feet of water on an east coast beach, they are essentially a winter, deep-water species. Much of the skill in taking the big catches of cod is due to the skipper of the boat, and not the individual angler. For it is the skipper, with his intimate knowledge of the surrounding marks, backed up by the very latest in electronic fish-finding gear, who really deserves the credit. All the fishermen does is wind them to the surface.

Having said that, it doesn't mean that there are no situations when the angler deserves any credit. It is just that a big cod shoal, located in deep water, is usually no problem to catch, whether on artificial lures or fish baits. On a charter boat full of anglers, there will always be an individual who has more than his share of good luck. As far as I am concerned, as regards the pursuit of any species, in freshwater or salt, the man who catches one single big fish is lucky. The angler who lands the most average-sized fish is a fully competent fisherman. Of course, as in any area, it is only the biggest, largest or strongest that attracts the most attention. What I have to say will not see you dragging a mammoth cod through the kitchen doorway but it might see you walking off the boat with a few cod every time you go fishing.

The first method of boat fishing is drifting. Used mostly in Scotland, Ireland and the West Country, it's a method that allows a good deal of ground to be covered with you going after the cod,

A 20 lb cod planes in the tidal flow after falling to a shiny pirk. Use a stiff rod when working the pirk.

rather than them coming to you. The reason drifting is employed appears to be two-fold. In the areas I have mentioned there are strong tides coupled with very rough ground in the shape of rocks and kelp beds. Anchoring would be successful, but for years the boats have drifted to avoid tackle losses at the bottom. Now of course they realise that while drifting over a specifically defined area can reap rewards, bottom fishing from an anchored boat will catch more. On the other hand if you are fishing a tractless void of sand or shingle, where the fish are likely to be spread out, then to drift the boat and thus cover a larger area is a positive advantage.

In the south-east corner of England where the cod run thick as bugs on a bumper in the months from October to January, the reverse is true. They anchor more than drift, and I suspect it is because the strong tides in that corner of the channel are so strong they are worried they will drift too far, too fast! There is only patchy rough ground here, and drifting seems an obvious method to me.

Boat Fishing

Both areas are steeped in the traditional methods of fishing the cod, which have always been, and always will be, a primary food source. But if you move slightly further north to the Essex coastline, you have clean sand and strong tides. This is surely an area where anglers could anchor to fish that are on the bottom. They do, but this small area almost revolutionised the art of fishing strong tides in shallow water by developing a method called uptiding. Which just goes to show that you don't always have to stick to one particular method, even if you are fishing in an area where it appears traditional. Having said that, after a decade of uptiding, we now have a breed of angler who is intent on traditionalising it! He appears over the deep water wrecks off the southern and south-western charter ports, and fishes away from the boat, casting uptide in over thirty fathoms of water! The advantage of this technique is then wasted, but there is no convincing a dyed-in-the-wool uptider that he is in water too deep to have any advantage.

Drifting

Of the three techniques I believe that in general drifting is the method least likely to produce a lot of good fish. When fish are thin on the ground you should use a drifting boat to locate them. If you are being pushed along by either tide or wind and the eight-ounce lead is bumping along nicely over the clean ground, you may take a fish. If you rebait and drop down again and take another fish as soon as the bait bumps along, the first thing you or the skipper should do, is take the bearings or Decca co-ordinates of the mark. Then go directly back into the direction of the drift and drop anchor. Why on earth just keep on drifting, *away* from where you have just hit fish? Even if you hit the odd fish again half a mile on, you really should be back up where the fish are shoaled thickest.

The echo sounder might show some sort of indentation or rock feature on the bottom. If it does you should be anchored upwind or uptide of it, so the baits drop back down to the feeding fish. In all the days I've drift fished around our coastline, I have never had a good haul of cod on a long drift. I think perhaps it is an easy way for the

Go Fishing for Cod

A big cod near the gaff as captor Tony Kirrage looks on. Fishing in deep water has seen many fish caught in the summer months when two decades ago they were thought to be only winter fish.

skipper to give his party a day afloat, but in this age of competition for bookings, such skippers soon fall by the wayside.

When drifting you need to remember just a couple of basic points. Use just enough lead to ensure you are bumping over the bottom, and adjust the length of your trace according to tidal conditions. Basically when you are drifting fast you can use a long flowing trace up to ten feet long. A double-hook rig with one hook at the end and another halfway up the trace allows you to use two different baits. As the drift increases in speed with tide or wind, add or remove lead to bump bottom. If you use too much lead a fish taking the bait may feel it and drop it. If you use too little the bait will rise up off the seabed and be dragging through at a height of several feet above the cod's feeding area. Remember that over such ground they are going to be feeding on the bottom.

You should use only a three-foot trace at slack water, or at the boat's slowest drifting speed, and lengthen it as the boat's speed picks up. Primary baits are strips of squid, herring or mackerel. I always anoint my baits with pilchard oil and you can add a flasher spoon uptrace of the bait. This is yet another technique that the cod angler should use, for it gives good results. I have already mentioned that I believe a feeding cod will take any small fish, not just winter whiting, and I am sure the dabs and immature flounders receive more than passing attention from big cod. If you've ever watched a film of a flatfish burying itself in the sand, or if you have seen a flounder spook in clear water while you are wading, you will have seen a mighty puff of sand which, to a passing cod, rings both the visual and the vibration dinner bell. When you rig a flasher spoon above the hook some anglers feel you stimulate either one sense in the cod or the other. Personally I believe they stimulate both, so every time you have a respectable drift going, try one.

There used to be a commercially produced flasher assembly that you could attach to your terminal rig, called a Rauto rig. It was very successful, but you can fashion your own quite easily. Remember you may hit some rough ground on the drift, and something expendable is preferable to a chunk of expensive shop-bought merchandise. A favourite is the bowl of a plastic table spoon, the type used as expendable cutlery by the catering trade. All you do then is snap the bowl of the spoon off where it meets the stem or handle, then make a hole through the lip of the spoon and attach a split ring. You will probably split the first couple of spoons where the plastic is brittle, so use either a fast drill with a fine drill bit, or melt a hole through using a heated nail. If the bowl is too scoop-shaped you can alter it by dropping it into some boiling water. This will warp it, but lift it out with pliers, drop it on the table, bowl up, and push a piece of wood down on the bowl to flatten it. Before it has cooled drop it into cold water to make it set in the required shape. Teaspoons can be used for small codling, but the larger tablespoon size is much better. There's no need to limit yourself to just one shape either. You can flatten or curve an ordinary piece of hard white plastic to flutter over the bottom. With the tablespoon you can use more than one 'blade', in fact I would advise three or four that will kick up tiny puffs of sand as they flutter their way over the seabed. This gives the appearance of a small flatfish trying to escape. A cod of even 10 lb will engulf the lot, bait, plastic spoons, swivels, and all! You can also use metal spoons, but plastic works better on a slow drift or in a weak tide.

The best distance to put the spoons from the bait varies from two feet uptrace of the hook, to clipped just above the bait. I like to rig them only three or four inches above the hook, as often the cod will make a grab for the flashing plastic as well as the bait. You might as well have a hook near both. The best bait to use in conjunction with a spoon rig is either squid or the belly strip of mackerel. Both are durable and withstand the attention of crabs well. The best way to fish spoons on the drift is to drop down until the lead hits bottom, then let out a further thirty yards of line so that it angles well away from the boat. Leave the reel out of gear but keep your thumb on the spool, and get used to the lead bumping over rock, sand, shingle and mud. The bite, when it comes, should be quite sharp, and with a reel out of gear you are free to give slack line immediately, allowing the fish to take the bait. Then, satisfied the fish has the bait, drop the reel into gear and set the hook. It sounds simple, but requires a little experience to differentiate the various types of ground on which you are fishing.

Another method of drifting when you are moving across rougher ground is jigging with feathers. In this technique a set of mackerel

Boat Fishing

Small boat cod supremo Norman Message shows off a pair of 20 pounders that fell to a slim line pirk designed for Sussex codding. Norman's boat *4 Pints* has seen some fantastic hauls of cod over the years, all taken mostly by himself and his sidekick, Bob Edwards.

flashers, or bigger cod feathers, is tied at the loop to your reel line. To the other end is tied the lead, and you drop the lot down until it hits bottom. Then you simply jig them up and down in a sweeping motion to simulate a school of tiny whitebait darting just off the seabed. When cod are thick on the ground, irrespective of their size, this method hauls them in one after the other. It is not exactly skilful, as jigging is about the oldest form of basic fishing technique you can get.

To add a bit of spice to this fairly monotonous routine, you can add a pirk in place of the lead. The pirk was probably popularised in Scotland and the north of England, where cod are a primary food fish. It can be purchased at a tackle shop for a few pounds, and consists of a mirrored length of chrome with a treble hook at one end. They are expensive to lose, especially as the pirk is continually hitting bottom. Most anglers make up their own from lengths of chrome tubing partially filled with lead. It has a flattened top end, with a slight bend in it to make it wobble and flutter as you jig it up and down.

In place of flashers or feathers you can use small imitation plastic squid, now popularised as 'muppets'. These come in a wide variety of colours and sizes, generally three on a trace, but they work better than ordinary white cod feathers, especially over wrecks. To spice them up even more you can incorporate a chemical lightstick called a Cyalume that is currently being used by American anglers for many deep-water species. This consists of two chemicals held together in a plastic phial. When the plastic is bent, it cracks one of the internal phials so that the two chemicals can mix, producing a vivid light. These are obtainable in many different sizes and colours, the best of which is the green or yellow 'lunker light'. They also do red and blue in larger sticks, giving 30 minutes of high intensity, or twelve hours of moderate light. They certainly add to the catch rate, although it's important to remember that you cannot get a fish to strike a lure if you aren't in the right place! When jigging with feathers, you can also add to your catch rate by putting a small fillet of mackerel on each hook bend. Very often this will provoke a response from the cod.

You will find extremely localised concentrations of cod when you are wreck fishing. You will find a high concentration of good-sized fish, clustered over the only feeding area for some distance. Most of

Boat Fishing

Yet another 20 lb plus cod for the author. Deep water wreck fishing ensures fish of this size and larger can be taken through the settled months of summer when distant marks can be safely reached.

the wrecks are within forty miles of our coastline, being casualties of the First and Second World Wars. Many naval and commercial ships were sunk in air and sea battles, targets of the highly successful U-boat submarine groups used by the Germans in the Second World War, which used to hunt in packs. Many of these submarines would lie in wait opposite a lighthouse or headland before a major shipping port, and silhouette their targets before sinking them.

Many of these freighters went down in one piece, and settled on the seabed with no rock or other structure for miles around them. In no time at all they became host to a wide variety of small crustaceans, with shrimps, crabs and prawns living in the sanctuary of the ships' hulls and superstructure. Weed grew on the hulls, and the smaller species of fish moved in to feed on the shrimps. The next step in the food chain were the larger fish, and the migratory cod soon cashed in on this regular source of food. These boats are likely to have been sunk between 10 and 30 miles offshore, in 40 fathoms or more of water, where the surrounding seabed is devoid of life. A huge ship's hulk stands out like an oasis on the seabed, and the fish live almost permanently around it.

The commercial trawlers cannot drag their nets too close to the hulk for fear of snagging them and losing all their gear. To avoid this, they have sophisticated electronic equipment that can pinpoint the exact position of the wrecks and allow the trawls to be fished around the edge. Occasionally a commercial ranges too close and loses his entire net, which of course gives further cover to all the fish living there.

Some ships were sunk in relatively shallow water or in a shipping lane, where they created a hazard to today's merchant and passenger vessels. Naval crews blew them apart with explosives, and the strong tides scattered them over a wider area. Nevertheless, they still represent good fishing areas, and are certainly worth visiting.

Many of these wrecks are fished so regularly by rod and line techniques that the boats have to move further and further offshore to find the fish. The northern method of jigging is probably still the most successful way of fishing a wreck, and for cod fishing, you should fish with the boat almost always on the drift. The sequence to follow is this. The skipper follows the bearings provided by his Decca Navigator equipment and locates the shape of the wreck with an echo sounder. He then drifts the boat so that the fishing lines drop down in front of the wreck, and drifts right over the superstructure itself. This is a lot higher than the surrounding seabed, so anglers not listening to what their skipper tells them will soon lose their end gear.

You can jig near the bottom, which is the best area for productive strikes, but when the skipper shouts that the wreck is coming, he means you to wind up a few turns so the baits or lures clear the superstructure of the ship. When your charter boat has drifted over the back of the wreck, you can of course drop back down to the clean ground in the lee of the hull.

To spice up the catch rate a bit, and to give you a chance of some better-sized fish, you could change from ordinary cod or heavy-duty mackerel feathers, to the plastic 'muppets' or plastic squid described previously. In place of the lead, you should put a long slim pirk with a treble hook at the end. You can even slide a larger plastic squid over the trebles, but I think that at these depths there will be little light penetration. Why not tip each hook of the treble with a slice of fresh mackerel. This adds scent to your rig, and may provoke a strike from ling or conger as well. With such low light penetration at these depths, it is worth mounting a cyalume chemical lightstick into, or onto, your pirk, in order to make it more visible to the fish. This way you have both scent and visual stimulators working for you. If it is swept up and down in a fairly violent action you also have vibration. You should be picking up fish every couple of drifts using this rig.

It's also possible to take them on bait, using a long flowing trace, with an entire calamari squid, or better still, a whole baby mackerel mounted on an 8/0 Partridge hook. Keep your lead only as heavy as you need to hold bottom, or at least to feel it bumping, and listen to the skipper or watch the echo sounder trace yourself, in order that you wind up off the seabed and avoid losing your gear as you drift over the superstructure. You can pick up better cod this way, certainly larger double-figure fish, but it's a risky method as you are living dangerously by dragging your bait over the bottom.

For some reason, possibly because of tidal conditions, the cod will be swimming in a shoal above the superstructure itself. I'm not sure if they are actually feeding when they do this, or whether they just hold station over the top of the wreck until the tide eases. However, ask any charter skipper and he will confirm that the cod shoals move to different parts of the wreck at different states of the tide. To capitalise on this, you should use a method generally used for pollock and coalfish. This is fishing with an artificial sandeel, where you drop down and retrieve constantly. You are searching for a fish that is holding station right above the wreck's superstructure, and therefore the chances of snagging are very high. You need to listen carefully for the exact moment when you should drop down or wind up, so that the fluttering action of the sandeel wags its way right through the middle of the shoal. Cod have a voracious appetite, so I would advise using the largest possible sandeel imitation you can buy. The best colours are yellow, orange or black.

'Muppets' will not produce nearly as well as they do when fished near the bottom, but try taking off the 'muppets' and using a pirk, either shop-bought or home-made, that has a fairly pronounced angle in it. This makes it flutter violently when worked. Drop this down while watching your boat's echo sounder, but do it from the opposite side of the boat to the drift. In other words, your line will be going under the boat slightly. There is then every chance that the pirk can actually be seen on the echo sounder, which of course allows you to stop it at just the depth the shoal is lying at. Put the reel in gear and start jigging it up and down. I have had cod grab the pirk the very instant I threw the reel in gear, purely because I had been able to stop the lure at the same depth the shoal was swimming at. Even if the main shoal of fish hasn't registered on the sounder, you can use this technique to get the pirk as close to the superstructure as possible, without too much risk of snagging up.

You can also get the odd fish to hit on a dour day, by what is called 'speedwinding' the pirk up. Drop down as usual, either until your pirk reaches the required depth, or until it hits bottom if you so wish. Drop the reel in gear, point the rod straight down the line and turn the reel handle like crazy. The cod will race up and crash the fluttering pirk in the first thirty turns. The only minor drawback with this technique is that it can be very tiring. Try it for three or four drifts, then go back to the slower redgill.

Anchoring

When anchoring, you will be looking for an area to fish that you are fairly sure is broken ground that cod may frequent. Having said that, once you have anchored the boat and dropped the bait down, you are very definitely waiting for the cod to come to you, rather than vice-versa. As much attention should be paid to the presentation of bait as when you are shore fishing, and although I have known catches from lures, I should put aside any thoughts of lure fishing at anchor. This is primarily a bait-fishing method, and some of the situations you come across may seem strange.

We already know that the cod like deep water, and they also like areas of strong tide to trundle food along the bottom. While you are not always going to be fishing in deep water, you will nearly always need a good tide running to fish this species effectively. We can divide anchoring for cod into two types, downtiding and uptiding.

Boat Fishing

The sun is shining, shirts are off and the cod are biting. Drift fishing for cod under these conditions is pleasant indeed.

Go Fishing for Cod

Downtiding is simply lowering your bait over the side. The tide pulls it away, then you drop the lead over, and lower everything to the seabed. The first thing to remember is not to drop the lead down too quickly, otherwise the trace will spiral upwards and twist round the main line. Once it has dropped out of sight, you simply have no way of knowing whether or not the rig is tangled. You may possibly get a bite like this, but any fish taking such a tangle is sure to miss the hook altogether, if it takes the bait at all! The idea is to use either a plastic or a metal Clement's boom, which allows the trace to travel down to the seabed about three inches away from the main line. When the lead hits the bottom the tide should pull the slower sinking bait at the end of the trace out straight. The smell and juices from that bait then percolate downtide on the current and attract any feeding cod.

You could make up your own Clement's booms from coat-hanger wire. Using a pair of cutters and pliers you can then make it to six inches or more long, which keeps the trace even further away from the main line and allows you to drop the bait down more quickly. This is important if the cod are known to have a relatively short feeding spell at a given state of the tide. As a rule of thumb, I always make the length of the trace longer, the harder the tide starts to run. At slack water, when the line is pretty well straight up and down, you can even rig a one-hook paternoster, or keep your running trace to two feet. As the tide begins to push, lengthen this to three, then four feet, finally going up to as much as ten feet when you are just managing to hold bottom.

In deep water downtiding like this, you must take into account the water pressure on the line, and also the angle at which the tide is pushing against it. Obviously if the tide is running hard you are going to need substantial weight to keep your line straight down, and any fish feeling the extra weight is unlikely to take the bait with confidence. That means you get a poor bite, and are more likely to miss it. With a shallower angle of line against the flow of the tide, you can use less lead, and therefore get a much more distinguishable bite. Another problem arises when the tide runs hard. Monofilament nylon line absorbs the 'feel' of the lead hitting bottom. It also bellies out into the tide and is slowly built up against the line until it lifts the

60

Boat Fishing

In Ireland the fish don't seem to run as big, possibly due to the slightly warmer sea temperature generated by the North Atlantic Drift. However, the author took this fine pair of double figure cod from George Burgum's Dingle-based boat *The Skua*. Bait was a belly strip of mackerel fished on a long flowing trace.

lead off the bottom. Many anglers swear they are definitely still on the bottom, but if you get them to put the reel in free spool, you can see the rod top kick as the lead runs back down to the sand again. All they do is sit there with a bait planing thirty feet off the bottom. While this only occurs when tidal flows reach their peak, it is worth remembering that you are missing out on the best of the fishing times!

To get the line angled back behind the boat you need to drop down until the lead hits the bottom, but keep the reel out of gear with your thumb on the spool. Allow fifteen or twenty seconds for the tide to belly the line back then sweep the rod up high, releasing the spool with your thumb when the rod is at its highest point. You will feel the line run out, and can actually feel the lead bump bottom. You should do this as many times as it takes to get the line at a shallow angle, and the bait way behind the stern of the boat. Then you can flip the reel back in gear and either hold the rod watching the tip, or put it down. I prefer to hold the rod, keeping the reel out of gear but holding the spool with my thumb. Then when I feel a fish take, I give him line straight away so he feels nothing out of the ordinary. When you are sure he has the bait well, hit him hard with the reel in gear. It may even pay to wind down fast to take the stretch out of the mono line before you hit him, thus thumping the hook well in. One of the best reels for this monofilament work is the Ryobi S320 Bigwater trolling reel. It has ample capacity, and plenty of reserve power in the star drag to cope with the twenty pounders.

In areas of exceptional tidal flow such as the Isle of Wight grounds and the Bristol Channel, you should try to acquaint yourself with the hooking properties of wire line. This can be either multi-strand, made by someone like Sevenstrand in America, or single-strand wire that used to be made by Berkley. You may have to shop around before you find a shop that stocks it, and it will be considerably more expensive than plain monofilament line. To house wire line you need a bigger reel, preferably with a level wind, and for this you will be hard pushed to better the Ryobi S340. This allows minimal coiling of the wire line, and spreads it evenly across the spool. If wire line kinks, even if you untwist it, it will still represent a weak spot. While I think a fish is unlikely to break it through pulling power, there may come a time when you get snagged in the bottom, and if you pull harder to free it, the wire will break at that kink. It's an expensive material to work with, and any loss should be kept to a minimum.

To avoid snagging up wire in the bottom, I use what I term a 'shocker' or rubbing trace at least twelve feet in length. This can be made of 30-lb monofilament, and attached to the wire line either by whipping or by a snap swivel. Then should the terminal tackle get snagged up in the bottom you can pull for a break, knowing that the nylon will break before the wire, thus saving the expense of purchasing more. Another word of caution here. Should you have the misfortune to get the wire itself snagged, on no account start coiling wraps of it around your fingers to pull it free. Wire line, both single-strand and braided, will act like a cheese cutter, and you can lacerate your fingers, or worse if the boat is drifting along and you can't get your hands free. It is better to take a piece of wood, wrap some rags around it, then coil a few overlapping turns of the offending wire around that. Take up as much tension as you can,

Boat Fishing

The gulls wheel in the afternoon winter sky as a big cod boils in the pull of the tide. If using wire line be careful to ease the fish in slowly. The non-stretch qualities of this line are excellent for bite detection but brute force can tear a hookhold free.

then get the skipper or a friend to add more tension below your handhold, but avoiding coiling the wire round any hands. Most wires should break out under this pressure.

The best advice I can give to users of wire line is to keep it under whenever you fish with it. Even when you wind the line back down through the rings at the end of the day, keep finger pressure on it and either tape the tag end to the reel spool, or put a wide elastic band around the spool to prevent it leaping off in coils. When you lower it to the seabed with the terminal tackle, ensure you do it at a steady, tensioned pace, stopping the reel spool the minute the lead hits bottom. You can still trot the terminal gear and bait back downtide, but do so keeping the rod top and lead in close contact. Remember with wire line you will need a fraction of the lead that the monofilament anglers are using, and therefore will not need to trot the bait so far back downtide to create a shallow angle of line for the water pressure to push against.

Finally, take it smooth and steady when you start to work on a hooked fish. There is no stretch in wire and you therefore impart any pressure from the bend of the rod directly to the fish below. It's all too easy to rip a hook out of the fish, or break a nylon trace. This happens whether the fish is near the boat and ready for gaffing, or just hooked and thrashing around like mad. You can use a longer length of rubbing or shock leader, but as monofilament is very stretchy it appears to offset the use of wire line.

Downtiding has been the classic way of taking cod for years, and the advent of wire line gave anglers the opportunity to fish new areas of strong tide previously unfishable, or allowed them to stay out in deep water and fish an entire tidal pattern through without having to re-anchor in a slacker area. I have to say that wire line has not really established itself with many anglers, largely, I fear, because people bought a spool, loaded a reel, and then didn't realise how to use it properly. Believe me, wire line will make a better fisherman of you, as you begin to appreciate the differences in bite detection. Then when you revert back to nylon line, you tend to stay in contact with the lead, and therefore the species, much better. But while wire lining is considered 'heavy' tackle fishing in deep water, you can also take cod around the Essex coast in water only thirty feet deep! Fishing is like

Crookhaven skipper, Bear Havinga, landed this haul of cod using rubber artificial eels while he drifted his boat off Mizen Head in south-west Ireland for Porbeagle shark, accompanied by the author. Ireland has had a prolific boom in cod catches over the last few years but rarely produces fish over 25 lb.

Even on a shark fishing trip the author couldn't resist having a drop with a fillet of mackerel. The result was this 10 lb cod taken on Alec Hicks's boat *Gloria*. They also landed three blue shark.

Norman Message with a cod that neared 30 lb. Fish of this size are fairly common in winter boat catches but rarer in summer dinghy catches.

A flood tide pushes up the shingle beach as top beach matchman Tony Kirrage keeps vigil for signs of a cod. With two fish already on the beach, chances are good that others will be around for the remainder of the tide.

Wrapped up against the November winds, the author swings in a plump codling, the first of a night session. Make sure you keep your lugworm out of the wind or frost or else they will freeze solid!

Take a cod from the shore and you have to be content. The author unhooks the first of his 1988 shore cod from Langney Point at Eastbourne.

A beaming smile says it all. Graeme Pullen with a good mixed bag of codling and big pout taken from a Sussex shore mark. Beach fishing for cod really does have a magic all of its own.

Winter brings the best of the cod fishing for the shore angler. By taking note of when the fish ran through on a previous tide, the author was able to capitalise on the next tide with this 18 fish catch from Trimingham Beach in Norfolk.

that, there are no hard and fast rules for taking fish regularly. The successful anglers adapt and change.

Downtiding can be reasonably successful in this shallow water, but somebody in touch with the refinements of uptiding will outfish them every time. To this day I cannot see why uptiding is so successful. After all, fishing is all about baits in the water, and you have the same baits with both techniques. Uptiding was born because some charter skippers operating in shallow water began thinking about what might put a fish off. Uptiding was not invented by any one person, it sort of 'appeared' before becoming accepted. It was probably used more than fifty years ago, and called something completely different, as there is nothing really new in fishing.

Basically it was thought that fish moving over the shallow offshore banks were very wary in such depths, and took baits fished directly behind the stern of the boat quite cagily. Perhaps this was due to the sound emanating from the water rushing against the side of the boat. Or it has been suggested that the continual thrumming sound coming from the anchor rope was transmitted across the seabed to tell fish to keep clear. I can't believe this myself. As an enthusiastic wire line angler, I have had the wire line making a high-pitched whine in a full bore tidal flow, and the fish were never put off by it. Wire would surely relay this sound down its length to the bait more easily than shock-absorbing monofilament. Could the sound of anglers walking about on deck be heard downtide by the fish? Did they shy away and avoid the fisherman's offering? It may be true of course, but I rather doubt it. We are fishing for wild creatures that probably have had no previous contact with man, and which 'hear' differently from us as well. That sound carries well through water is a scientific fact, but I cannot believe it deters them.

My own, possibly unusual, theory is as follows. When fishing downtide, all the anglers on the boat will be dropping their baits over the side bouncing them back downtide. It doesn't matter how far back those baits are fished from the boat, they will be spaced no further apart than the width of the stern, which is very narrow on some boats. The smell from those baits will be travelling downtide, and will be long and narrow, the width of the boat in fact. Any fish passing over that 'smell lane' will be likely to follow it uptide to its source. The source, as far as the fish is concerned will probably be the bait fished furthest away from the boat. This is why the boat positions at the stern are generally the more productive to fish from. If you cast your baits away from the side of the boat, on either side, you are making that 'smell lane' much wider, and it will therefore draw more fish to the area. The smell itself will of course be less concentrated, but spread over a wider area, and it will mean that the bait cast far out from the side of the boat will have as much chance of being taken as the one fished directly downtide of the stern.

If you cast from the side of the boat, you have the added problem that the tide will be pushing against the line from an angle broadside to the boat, which will of course mean that the bait cannot hold bottom, and will be dragged round to the stern. You can add lead, but you reach a stage when you cannot possibly cast 2lb of lead while using a 50-lb shark rod! There needs to be a happy medium, and this problem is overcome by applying a piece of equipment used by the shore angler. Simply attach a nose-wired lead or break-out lead to your terminal gear, and replace the running leger rig of downtide fishing with the fixed paternoster of the beach angler. The actual snood needs to be lengthened from 18 inches to four feet or more, but the hook can be looped onto the wire of the lead so that it comes free on impact with the water and floats free down the current. With weight ranges reduced from $1^1/4$ lb downtide to 6 oz for uptiding, there is an increase in the sport when you hook a fish.

You needn't necessarily cast the lead at 90 degrees to the side of the boat. Throw it slightly downtide or uptide to space them out. As soon as the lead hits water you must let it fall free to the bottom, unhindered except for a light thumbing of the reel spool to prevent an overrun. As soon as the lead hits, allow several yards of loose line to belly into the tide before dropping the reel into gear. This allows the tide to press on the line and in attempting to pull the lead downtide, will pull the grips of the wired lead in to the seabed. The bait is then firmly anchored down and the cod can home in on the scent trail emanating from it.

Now the fishing is exactly the same as for the shore fisherman who casts a bait from a steep shingle beach in an area of strong tide. The cod comes along, picks up the bait, and attempting to move away, comes up tight against the grip lead. This makes it panic slightly and it bolts, which pulls the grip lead free, while pulling the hook partially in to the barb. It is almost a self-hooking device.

At the angler's end, he will see the rod top bowed over under the pressure of the tide acting against the line. The cod comes along, and picks up the bait, giving a slight nod on the rod top. As he bolts, so the angler's rod kicks down and then falls slack as the cod careers downtide, towing the grip lead behind it. Usually it will be hooked anyway, but reel all the bow and stretch out of the line before setting the hook, hard, two or three times. There is no need for wire line here. You need a good quality nylon line like Sylcast or Ande, in the 15-lb range, with a heavier beachcasting reel, and a special uptiding rod. This will be longer than the standard boat rod, designed not only to cast, but to pull over progressively in the flow of tide, and 'ease' the grip wires into the sand. A stiff rod would drag them out if the boat rocked.

Uptiding is very successful in shallow areas of 20 feet or less, and drops off in productivity the deeper you go. There would be little point in uptiding in thirty fathoms of water for instance. The time taken for the lead to reach bottom would see it swing back under the hull, and the advantage of getting a bait away from the boat would be lost. You can also see that there would be no place for wire line in the shallow water, as it is difficult if not impossible to cast and fish too close to the boat in such shallow depths. Baits for uptiding are generally worms and peeler crabs, with eel tails and strips of herring, mackerel and squid running a close second. Instead of the larger fish baits of downtiding techniques, the uptider should look to big bunches of lugworm, threaded up the hook and over the eye, with a whole peeler crab as secondary bait.

Above: The art of uptiding for cod has proved popular with the dinghy angler. In a restricted space, this technique enables the angler to use several rods without any risk of the lines crossing and causing a tangle.

Below: One of the best baits for a big cod is a whole squid mounted on a large single hook as shown here.

A prime cod in the peak of condition and a standard size for the uptiding specialists. As the saying goes, 'They fight all the way to the frying pan!'

Tackle

It is rare that two anglers can agree on which tackle is best for a given situation. My own tackle comes under the heading of essential, but just enough to do the job. I put more faith in being able to locate the fish in the first place than I do in posing up and down the beach, with the latest in shore fishing gadgetry! The same goes for boat anglers. Many of them like to be seen with the 'right' tackle, which gives the impression that they are highly advanced anglers who know what they are doing. What follows is not a list of the latest multi-gimmick fishing tools. It is a list of tried and tested quality equipment that has the reputation of advanced technology, without all the sales frills. Cod are basic creatures, and although bulky and heavy, they are unlikely to rip 300 yards of line against ten pounds of drag, leap ten feet and throw the squid back at you! The fight with this species is sluggish and heavy, but they grow to a very good size, and for many anglers are the largest fish they may catch.

Rods need to be strong, not especially for the weight of the fish, but for the fishing conditions and amount of lead you use. A shore fisherman needs a standard twelve-foot beachcaster with enough backbone to throw a six-ounce lead at least a hundred yards. The 2600 Conoflex range offered by Michael McManus fit the bill nicely, and they are possibly the most popular cod blank in use today. As I have said, the object for the average angler is not to throw the lead to America, but to put a correctly presented bait around 70 yards out; more if you can achieve it comfortably. Rings need to be Fuji, there is

One of the south coast's top shore matchmen, Tony Kirrage, leader of Tony's Tackle Team, looks pleased with this brace of Sussex Cod taken on lugworm.

little point in using any other. For shore fishing you need a beach rest. This can be a single-leg monopod type, a tripod, or simply two pieces of wood screwed together with the rod itself making the third leg. It may pay you later to get a tripod for rock fishing or piers, and a monopod for the beach. The extra height offered by the latter gets the line up out of the wave line and may help your grip lead to hold out in rough conditions.

The best beach reels are made by Abu, but they are more of a casting reel than a heavy-duty fishing tool. The 6500 and 7000 models will suffice for most work, but the latest from the stable of Shimano look like being better. The Speedmaster is compact, strong and has a line-gobbling gear ratio that allows you to get the terminal gear up off the bottom quickly when rough ground fishing. I would also recommend the Ryobi T2 as among the better beach reels, it has a good gear retrieve ratio and casts smoothly. I think the T2 fits the average hand better than the Speedmaster, and also has a level wind for beginners.

As for lines, the Ryobi stable have their own brand of green monofilament in 15 lb. I see little point in dropping to anything less. Also excellent is the American Ande and Du Pont's Stren. You'll need a shock leader of between 35 lb for standard layback casting and 50 lb for pendulum styles. Many anglers use the gold-coloured Stren because it shows up well, and is very limp for its diameter.

You need to get shore hooks from your local tackle shop. The make I use is Partridge of Redditch, who make more patterns than you would ever use. Each bait requires a different-shaped hook. Worms need a long shank with a narrow gape, while bulky baits like peeler crab need a standard length shank but a wider gape so the hookpoint is not smothered. While you can get away with a fine wire Aberdeen blued hook for small codling on a open surf beach, you need a thick wire hook when fishing rough ground. A few anglers I know prefer a springy hook for rough ground work. When they get snagged up, careful handling will allow the hook to spring free, but it will not open up when a fish is being landed. Ask for the Partridge catalogue, or contact Alan Bramley the Managing Director if you have a specific request. He will do all he can to assist in the correct pattern of hook, and the size.

Tackle

The tide floods in and a cod already hangs on the author's beach rest. Waxham beach in Norfolk – the venue for some fine shallow water codding in December.

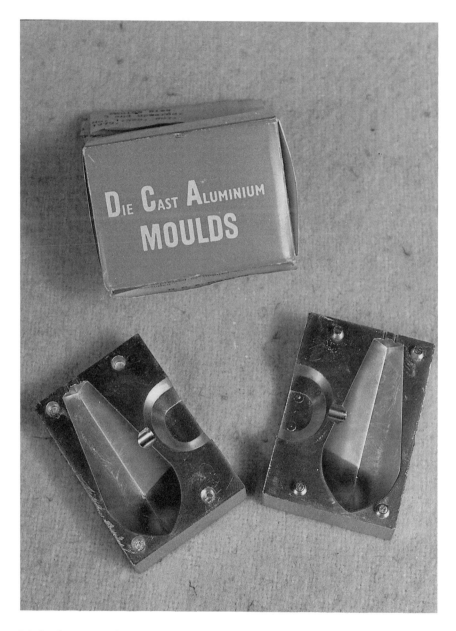

It is far cheaper to make your own leads from moulds than always buying them from the tackle shops – especially if you fish a snaggy stretch of coastline.

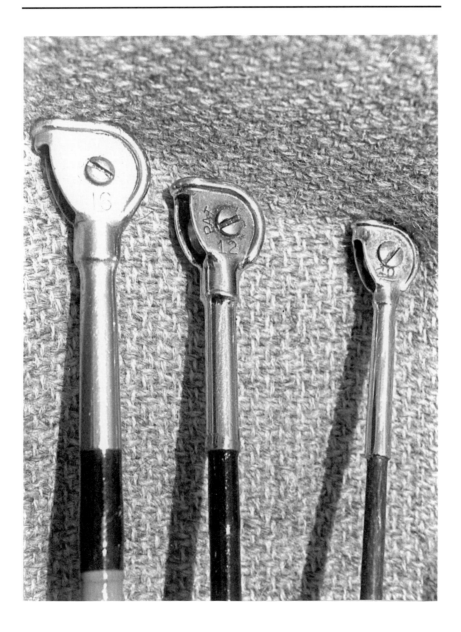

Wire line in boats will necessitate a roller tip ring like these. It minimises wearing through friction and makes playing a fish that much easier.

Go Fishing for Cod

For night fishing you are going to need illumination of some sort. A headlamp with battery pack is good for baiting up and landing fish, while background lighting should be from a pressure lamp. I still have one of the original Anchor lamps I bought from Tony's Tackle down in Eastbourne, and with a few services it has given me no problems. You can light them with the pre-heat burner, but this uses quite a bit of paraffin. Try to wait for the methylated spirits to do the pre-heating for you. It may save you a bit of fuel if you are out on a mammoth night session.

You can buy leads from your local tackle dealer, but most shore anglers make their own. All you need is a selection of moulds from Glyn Evans at DCA Moulds, and you can start your own production line. Make some as plain bombs and some with wire grips. I get my wire for this job from the model shop, and use the 18-swg wire used for the undercarriages. You can pre-drill holes in the moulds to take these wires and use elastic bands to hold them in place.

Baitclips can be purchased at the tackle shops or made yourself. All you need is some electric flex with the copper core removed, and some wire from paperclips. Make most of your hook snoods from at least 20 lb, as the cod won't be wary, and the stiffer mono of 20 lb will stop the hook line swinging round the main line and tangling.

Boat fishing is divided into two types, downtiding and uptiding. For downtiding you need a 20-lb or 30-lb class boat rod, again Conoflex make the best for British waters, and get one fitted out either with Aftco rollers throughout, or at the bare minimum, an Aftco roller tip, and Fuji intermediates. This will allow you to use wire line if you wish. The roller guides will reduce normal monofilament line friction against the rings, and give your line a longer life.

Ryobi make a red 30-lb line that wears well, and Slycast is very hard-wearing and has a reputation for taking many big fish. Ande and Stren have a good range, but try the Ande premium in 20-lb and 30-lb classes if you get a chance. Ryobi make a new line of reels, ideal for boat fishing like this. Called Big Water trolling reels, they have a star drag, good gear ratio, and plenty of line capacity. The SL 340 looks to be the best for wire line fishing, but the S320 can be used for monofilament work. Berkley in America used to make a single-strand

Tackle

For uptiding boat techniques you need a good through action rod like the one being used here by Littlehampton skipper, Bill Hunter. This enables you to cast comfortably but still get a satisfying fight when you do hook up a fish.

It is sensible to equip yourself with adequate lighting if you intend beach fishing at night. A hand torch, a headlamp or a paraffin pressure lamp are all perfectly adequate.

The use of fine wire Aberdeen hooks works well for shore cod of this size. For anything larger, or in areas of snags, go for a hook with a stronger wire that is less likely to spring open under pressure.

87

wire which had a thick diameter, but which may now be discontinued. At present, the best wire comes from Sevenstrand, who unknown to most British anglers make a tremendous range of wire line products. Admittedly designed for trace work and deep-water trolling, it is still highly effective for bottom fishing in strong tidal conditions. They make a stainless steel wire in 300-foot, 600-foot and 1000-foot spools, so it may pay you to team up with someone, buy a bulk spool and share the cost between you. Sevenstrand also offer nylon-covered stainless steel wire in 100, 300, 600 and 1000-foot spools. If you can't get any from your local tackle dealer, try Sevenstrand Tackle Corp, 5401 McFadden Avenue, Huntingdon Beach, CA 92649, U.S.A.

For downtiding you will need less lead, but Glyn Evans at DCA Moulds can give you some new boat moulds, with all shapes from bombs to heavy cones. All you need is the scrap lead to melt down. The best cod hooks are made by Mustads, who make thousands of different patterns, far too many for me to list here. Your tackle shop will best advise you on size, quantity and patterns, but keep to the strong wire category, as the cod in deep water are likely to run to a good size.

For uptiding, you need a lighter, longer rod than for downtiding, as it will be required to cast grip leads up to eight ounces in weight. The British company of North-Western market good uptiding blanks made from a carbon kevlar mix. These cast well, have plenty of backbone, yet retain a degree of flexibility to show what is happening to the bait below. Reels should either be similar to the Ryobi S320, or the Abu range, like the 7000 and 9000, which take plenty of 15-lb or 20-lb line and can cast well. Under certain conditions you can drop line strengths to 12 lb or less, but I never see the point in this as many anglers fail to realise they are pulling no harder with 20-lb test, than they do with 12 lb. Therefore nothing is to be gained, but you risk losing an extra large fish that picks up the bait with the light line attached to it!

Once you have set yourself up with this sort of tackle, your main aim should be to gain experience in the habits of the fish themselves. Cod are our premier food fish, and they represent a good fish to catch from both shore and boat. Good hunting!

COD, Atlantic

LINE CLASS WORLD RECORDS

LINE CLASSES	WEIGHT	PLACE	DATE	ANGLER
MEN				
2 lb	11.70 kg (25 lb 12 oz)	Helsingborg, Sweden	Aug. 21, 1986	H. Jacob Nyholm
4 lb	15.35 kg (33 lb 13 oz)	Helsingborg, Sweden	Aug. 20, 1986	Peter Madholm
8 lb	18.37 kg (40 lb 8 oz)	Cashes Ledge, New Hampshire, USA	Aug. 8, 1983	Robert H. Withee
12 lb	24.94 kg (55 lb)	Plum Island, Massachusetts, USA	July 6, 1958	W. C. Dunn
16 lb	24.49 kg (54 lb)	New Scantum, New Hampshire, USA	Oct. 15, 1983	Robert H. Withee
20 lb	44.79 kg (98 lb 12 oz)	Isle of Shoals, New Hampshire, USA	June 8, 1969	Alphonse J. Bielevich
30 lb	36.74 kg (81 lb)	Brielle, New Jersey, USA	March 15, 1967	Joseph Chesla
50 lb	38.55 kg (85 lb)	Montauk Point, New York, USA	Feb. 25, 1984	Frederick Shay, Jr.
80 lb	Vacant	Minimum Weight–34.01 kg (75 lb)		
WOMEN				
2 lb	7.82 kg (17 lb 4 oz)	Marblehead, Massachusetts, USA	Nov. 20, 1983	Mrs. Lillian D. LaBrie
4 lb	9.41 kg (20 lb 12 oz)	Middlebank, Massachusetts, USA	April 12, 1986	Mrs. Lillian D. LaBrie
8 lb	7.96 kg (17 lb 9 oz)	Freeport, New York, USA	Jan. 7, 1976	Mrs. Ronnie DeLuca
12 lb	15.42 kg (34 lb)	Middlebank, Massachusetts, USA	April 19, 1980	Mrs. Lillian D. LaBrie
16 lb	Vacant	Minimum Weight–11.33 kg (25 lb)		
20 lb	32.43 kg (71 lb 8 oz)	Cape Cod, Massachusetts, USA	Aug. 2, 1964	Muriel Betts
30 lb	28.63 kg (63 lb 2 oz)	Georges Bank, New York, USA	June 12, 1985	Ann Houseknecht
50 lb	34.13 kg (75 lb 4 oz)	Perkins Cove, Ogunquit, Maine, USA	June 18, 1984	Marjory Kerr
80 lb	37.08 kg (81 lb 12 oz)	Middlebank, Massachusetts, USA	Sept. 24, 1970	Mrs. Sophie Karwa

Reproduced by kind permission of IGFA (USA), Director of Operations, Mr Michael Leech.

A GUIDE TO COD FISHING HOOKS

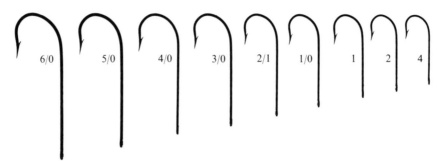

6/0 5/0 4/0 3/0 2/1 1/0 1 2 4

COX & RAWLE ABERDEEN HOOKS

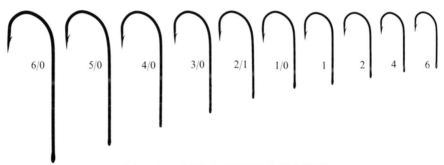

6/0 5/0 4/0 3/0 2/1 1/0 1 2 4 6

COX & RAWLE UPTIDE HOOKS

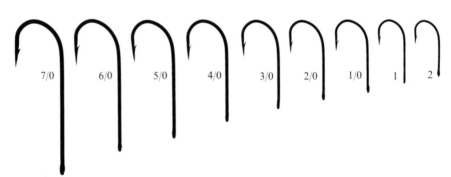

7/0 6/0 5/0 4/0 3/0 2/0 1/0 1 2

COX & RAWLE UPTIDE EXTRA HOOKS

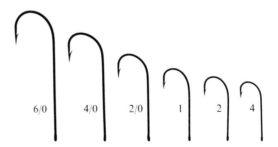

6/0 4/0 2/0 1 2 4

PARTRIDGE JOHN HOLDEN HOOKS

Hooks not to size.

Reproduced by kind permission of Mr Alan Bramley of Partridge of Redditch.

GO FISHING FOR

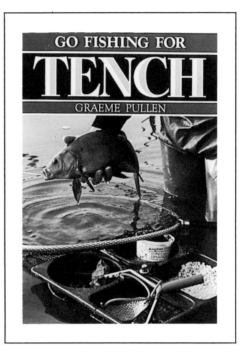

All available in the same series at £9.95 each.

96pp, 240 x 172mm
16pp colour and approx. 30 black & white photographs.

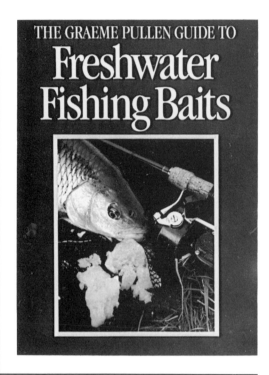